AI Insight: Navigating with Microsoft's Copilot

Part 1: Introduction

Contents

Introduction to Microsoft Copilot

This part of the book dives deep into what Microsoft Copilot is and how it can revolutionize your work with Microsoft 365 applications.

Chapter 1: What is Microsoft Copilot?

This chapter introduces you to the core concept of Microsoft Copilot. We'll explore:

- **1.1 Key Features and Benefits:** We'll delve into the functionalities that make Copilot a game-changer. This includes exploring its ability to:
  - Assist with writing, editing, and summarizing documents across various applications.
  - Generate creative content ideas and suggestions.

- Automate repetitive tasks and streamline workflows.

- Enhance data analysis and visualization in spreadsheets.

- Improve communication and collaboration within teams.

- **1.2 Understanding AI-Driven Functionality:**

We'll unpack the magic behind the scenes. This chapter will explain:

- The power of Artificial Intelligence (AI) that drives Copilot's suggestions and assistance.

- How Copilot learns from your work style and data to personalize its recommendations.

o The concept of Large Language Models
(LLMs) and their role in Copilot's
functionality.

Chapter 2: Getting Started with Copilot

This chapter equips you with the knowledge to get up and running with Copilot seamlessly. We'll cover:

- **2.1 System Requirements and Compatibility:** We'll identify the essential hardware and software needed to utilize Copilot effectively. This includes information on:
    - Operating system compatibility.
    - Hardware specifications for optimal performance.
    - Compatibility with different versions of Microsoft 365.

- **2.2 User Interface and Interaction:** We'll guide you through the user interface, making you comfortable navigating Copilot's features. This chapter will explore:

  - How to access and activate Copilot within different Microsoft 365 applications.

  - Understanding the layout and functionalities of the Copilot interface.

  - Utilizing various features like content suggestions, editing tools, and automation options.

- **2.3 Data Privacy and Security:** We'll address your concerns about data privacy and security. This chapter will explain:

- How Microsoft safeguards your information while using Copilot.

- The level of user control over the data Copilot utilizes.

- Best practices for maintaining data privacy while working with Copilot.

By the end of Part 1, you'll have a solid understanding of Microsoft Copilot's capabilities and be prepared to leverage its power in the following sections of the book.

Part 2: Copilot Across Microsoft 365 Applications

This part showcases the transformative power of Copilot in each core Microsoft 365 application. We'll explore how Copilot tailors its assistance to unlock the full potential of each program.

Chapter 3: Copilot in Word: Enhanced Document Creation

Struggling to overcome writer's block or generate fresh ideas? This chapter dives into how Copilot can revolutionize your writing experience in Word. We'll cover:

- **3.1 Overcoming Writer's Block and Generating Content:** Learn how Copilot can help you:

- Brainstorm outlines and generate content based on keywords or prompts.

- Overcome writer's block with suggested sentence starters and paragraph continuations.

- Paraphrase existing text or rephrase sentences for improved clarity.

- **3.2 Research Assistance and Intelligent Citations:** Discover how Copilot streamlines research and citation processes:

  - Conduct web searches and integrate relevant information directly into your document.

  - Generate citations in various academic styles (APA, MLA, Chicago) automatically.

- Fact-check information and ensure the credibility of your sources.

- **3.3 Formatting and Editing Support:** Effortlessly maintain a polished look and error-free writing with Copilot's assistance:

  - Utilize real-time grammar and style suggestions to improve sentence structure and flow.

  - Ensure consistent formatting throughout your document with automated tools.

  - Generate professional-looking tables of contents, indexes, and references.

Chapter 4: Copilot in Excel: Powerful Data Analysis

Unleash the full potential of your data with Copilot's intelligent tools in Excel. This chapter explores:

- **4.1 Data Exploration and Visualization Tools:** Gain deeper insights from your data:
    - Leverage Copilot's suggestions for data exploration techniques like pivot tables and charts.

- Visualize complex data sets with recommended charts and graphs tailored to your information.

- Uncover hidden trends and patterns within your data through Copilot's analysis.

- **4.2 Automating Calculations and Formulas:** Save time and minimize errors with Copilot's automation features:

  - Automate repetitive calculations and formula generation based on existing patterns.

  - Utilize Copilot's suggestions for complex formulas to streamline data analysis.

  - Clean and organize your spreadsheets with Copilot's help.

- **4.3 Creating Charts and Reports with Copilot:**

Generate impactful presentations of your data:

  - Craft compelling charts and graphs with Copilot's design recommendations.

  - Effortlessly create data-driven reports with automated formatting and data integration.

  - Communicate your findings effectively with visually appealing presentations.

Chapter 5: Copilot in PowerPoint: Streamlined

Presentations

Design professional and engaging presentations with minimal effort using Copilot in PowerPoint. This chapter will detail:

- **5.1 Design Inspiration and Slide Generation:**

  Get a creative head start:

- Generate design ideas and brainstorm slide layouts based on your presentation topic.
- Utilize Copilot's suggestions for multimedia integration like images and videos.
- Ensure a consistent and visually appealing presentation style with Copilot's design guidance.

- **5.2 Data Integration and Storytelling Techniques:** Transform data into a compelling narrative:
  - Integrate charts, graphs, and data visualizations seamlessly into your slides.

- Craft a clear and impactful story with Copilot's suggestions for slide transitions and storytelling techniques.

- Engage your audience with a well-structured and informative presentation.

- **5.3 Collaboration Features and Audience Engagement:** Facilitate a smooth and interactive presentation experience:

  - Work collaboratively on presentations with real-time co-editing features within Copilot.

  - Integrate audience participation tools like polls and Q&A sessions with Copilot's guidance.

- Deliver a memorable and impactful presentation that resonates with your audience.

This structure continues for the remaining chapters, outlining the functionalities of Copilot in Outlook, Teams, and other Microsoft 365 applications.

Chapter: Advanced Functionality of Copilot for Business and Personal Productivity

Microsoft's Copilot is one of the most advanced AI integrations in productivity software, bridging the gap between complex tasks and efficient execution. As organizations adopt artificial intelligence for various purposes, tools like Copilot stand at the intersection of user empowerment and technological enhancement. In this chapter, we'll explore how Copilot elevates business and personal productivity by providing intelligent automation, content creation assistance, and decision-making support, among other capabilities.

Enhancing Document Creation and Management

At its core, Copilot is designed to assist users in managing and creating content in a more efficient way. For business professionals, this means having the ability to draft emails, reports, presentations, and other documents faster than ever before. Copilot is integrated into Microsoft 365 apps, such as Word, Excel, PowerPoint, and Outlook, allowing users to generate tailored content, summarize lengthy documents, and even suggest improvements.

In Microsoft Word, Copilot can take raw text or bullet points and transform them into coherent paragraphs, offering suggestions for improved tone, clarity, and structure. This functionality is a game-changer for teams that need to quickly produce high-quality documentation, proposals, or marketing content. For business executives or content creators who may face writer's block or time constraints, Copilot can significantly reduce the effort needed to produce polished written material.

Powerful Data Analysis and Reporting

For many businesses, data-driven decisions are essential. Microsoft Copilot, with its integration into Excel, is especially beneficial for professionals who need to analyze large datasets and generate reports quickly. Copilot allows users to ask natural language questions about their data—something that would traditionally require advanced knowledge of data manipulation and formulas. A user might simply type, "What are the trends in sales over the last quarter?" and Copilot would not only identify the relevant data points but also generate insightful visualizations like graphs or tables.

For businesses working in complex industries such as finance, marketing, or operations, this is an invaluable tool. It lowers the barriers to data analytics by providing intuitive, user-friendly tools that enable employees of all technical levels to perform advanced analyses and gain actionable insights without needing deep expertise in data science.

Improving Communication Efficiency

In the realm of communication, Microsoft Copilot is transforming how professionals interact with one another through Outlook and Teams. With its smart email categorization and response suggestions, Copilot can prioritize emails, generate replies, and even draft meeting agendas. It analyzes patterns in your previous communication and ensures that your responses are aligned with your tone and messaging style. This can significantly reduce the time spent on email management, leaving professionals with more time to focus on high-value tasks.

In Microsoft Teams, Copilot helps streamline collaboration. Whether scheduling meetings, summarizing meeting notes, or generating follow-up tasks, Copilot can enhance how teams work together. For instance, if a meeting is recorded, Copilot can extract key takeaways, highlight action items, and assign tasks based on the conversation. This functionality aids in minimizing the need for manual note-taking and ensures that everyone is aligned on their responsibilities.

Task Automation and Process Improvement

Beyond document creation and communication, Copilot enhances productivity through automation. Many business processes, from customer service to inventory management, involve repetitive tasks that can be automated with the help of AI. Copilot's ability to understand workflows and offer recommendations for automating mundane tasks is invaluable for businesses aiming to optimize operations and reduce human error.

For example, a company's sales team can use Copilot to automate lead qualification by integrating data from their CRM. Copilot could assess potential leads based on pre-set criteria and automatically initiate the follow-up process, creating personalized emails and tracking responses. Similarly, for HR professionals, Copilot could automate candidate screening by analyzing resumes against job requirements, significantly reducing the time spent on manual review.

Decision-Making Support

Copilot's ability to assist in decision-making is one of its standout features. With its integration into tools like Excel and Power BI, users can generate insights that help guide business strategy. By analyzing data trends, market conditions, and historical performance,

Copilot offers predictive analytics and forecasts that can influence decisions ranging from resource allocation to product launches.

In the context of large organizations or corporations, decision-making often involves multiple stakeholders, a wealth of data, and many competing priorities. Copilot helps streamline this process by organizing data and presenting it in a clear, actionable format, enabling decision-makers to quickly understand the implications of their choices. Whether it's predicting customer behavior, recommending operational improvements, or suggesting cost-saving measures, Copilot empowers users with data-driven intelligence to make informed decisions faster.

Personal Productivity and Time Management

While Copilot is a powerful tool for businesses, it also has immense potential for individual productivity. For personal use, Copilot can manage schedules, assist in organizing tasks, and help prioritize day-to-day activities. By analyzing your calendar and communication, Copilot can suggest optimal times for meetings, block out focus time, and even offer reminders for upcoming deadlines.

Copilot's integration with personal apps and devices further enhances productivity by creating a seamless experience. For instance, syncing Copilot with your mobile device allows it to assist in email management, note-taking, and even offering personalized suggestions based on your recent activities or meetings. By offloading repetitive or time-consuming tasks, Copilot provides individuals with more bandwidth to focus on creative and strategic work.

Cognitive Load Reduction

One of the most powerful ways Copilot improves productivity is by reducing cognitive load. With the constant influx of information, tasks, and responsibilities, professionals often experience mental fatigue. Copilot helps alleviate this by taking over repetitive and time-consuming tasks, freeing up mental resources for more complex and creative problem-solving. By understanding natural language and anticipating the needs of users, Copilot significantly reduces the mental energy required to manage work tasks, which leads to greater focus and less burnout.

In the workplace, where multitasking is often a necessity, Copilot can help prevent the cognitive overload that typically results from juggling multiple projects. Whether it's generating reports, managing emails, or creating presentations, Copilot takes care of the mundane tasks, allowing individuals to spend their time on higher-order, strategic thinking.

Future Implications of Copilot's Functionality

The capabilities discussed so far are just the beginning of what Copilot can achieve. As Microsoft continues to improve its AI models and deepen integration across various Microsoft 365 apps, Copilot's functionality will only become more sophisticated. Future updates may include more advanced predictive capabilities, deeper contextual understanding of user needs, and seamless integration with external tools and services, further enhancing the ways in which individuals and organizations can achieve greater productivity.

Furthermore, as Copilot adapts to an organization's workflows and individual preferences over time, its recommendations and actions will become more tailored and efficient. With ongoing advancements in natural language processing, machine learning, and AI ethics, the potential for Copilot to transform business productivity is limitless. Organizations can look forward to increasingly personalized, intuitive, and

powerful assistance that enhances both individual and

team performance.

Chapter: Integration with Microsoft 365 Suite and Other Microsoft Technologies

Microsoft Copilot's value proposition is truly realized when it integrates seamlessly into the Microsoft 365 ecosystem, which includes essential productivity tools like Word, Excel, PowerPoint, Outlook, and Teams. Its deep integration within these tools transforms them from simple applications into powerful AI-powered assistants that help users accomplish tasks faster and more efficiently. Beyond Microsoft 365, Copilot extends its functionality into other Microsoft technologies, creating a unified ecosystem where users can maximize productivity with minimal effort.

Seamless Integration with Word, Excel, and PowerPoint

The integration of Copilot into Microsoft Word, Excel, and PowerPoint goes far beyond the automation of basic tasks. In Word, for instance, Copilot doesn't just auto-generate content, it can also reformat entire documents, generate citations, and assist in rewriting for clarity or tone adjustment. This deep integration allows users to quickly produce high-quality documents tailored to their needs. Copilot's natural language processing capabilities allow it to understand the context of a document, ensuring that the content fits the style and purpose intended by the user.

In Excel, Copilot takes data manipulation to new heights. It enables users to conduct complex analyses simply by asking questions in natural language. Instead of writing complex formulas, users can ask Copilot to "summarize last quarter's sales by region" or "highlight any sales outliers in the dataset." Copilot will parse through the data, provide a concise summary, and even create charts or tables that visually represent the data, all without requiring any technical expertise. The result is that employees, even those without a deep understanding of data science, can leverage powerful analytics to make informed decisions.

Similarly, Copilot in PowerPoint elevates the presentation creation process by generating slides based on the content from other documents. It can convert text into bullet points, suggest slide designs, and even draft speaker notes. This makes it easier for professionals to create presentations that are not only well-structured but also visually appealing, all with minimal manual input.

Enhancing Collaboration in Microsoft Teams

Collaboration in the modern workplace often requires managing multiple threads of communication simultaneously, making it easy to lose track of critical discussions. Microsoft Teams, with the addition of

Copilot, transforms how teams collaborate by providing intelligent suggestions and assistance across chats, meetings, and document sharing.

In meetings, Copilot can summarize key discussion points, create action items, and even suggest next steps based on the conversation. This helps ensure that meeting participants leave with a clear understanding of their tasks without having to manually sift through meeting notes. Copilot also integrates with Microsoft Teams' chat, offering quick replies and summarizations that help maintain the flow of conversation.

One of the standout features of Copilot in Teams is its ability to assist in scheduling. By analyzing past communications and calendar data, Copilot can suggest optimal meeting times, automatically considering participants' availability and workload. This minimizes the back-and-forth scheduling that often disrupts productivity and helps teams focus on more valuable tasks.

Integration with OneDrive and SharePoint for Document Management

In addition to the core productivity tools, Copilot enhances document management by integrating with OneDrive and SharePoint. These platforms are often central to how organizations store and share documents, and Copilot can help manage them by automatically categorizing files, suggesting relevant documents, and even recommending edits.

For instance, if a user is working on a project and needs to quickly locate supporting documentation, Copilot can search through the user's OneDrive or SharePoint and present the most relevant files. Additionally, Copilot's ability to suggest document revisions based on the context of a given task can improve collaboration and ensure that documents are always up-to-date.

Streamlining Workflow Automation through Power Automate

While Microsoft 365 apps themselves are powerful, Copilot's true strength emerges when it is used in tandem with Microsoft's broader suite of tools. Power Automate, a service that allows users to create automated workflows between different apps and services, becomes even more potent when integrated with Copilot.

With Copilot, users can automate repetitive tasks that span multiple platforms, such as sending personalized follow-up emails after meetings, managing data flow between Excel and Power BI, or automatically posting content to a team's social media channels. Instead of having to learn complex automation processes, Copilot enables users to create workflows with simple commands in natural language. A user might say, "Create an automated workflow to email the sales team every Monday with a summary of this week's performance," and Copilot will handle the rest.

Power Automate, combined with Copilot's AI capabilities, reduces the friction between different tools and apps, making cross-platform workflows seamless. This integration is especially useful for businesses that use a wide range of Microsoft tools, ensuring that all their systems communicate efficiently and with minimal manual effort.

Linking Copilot with Azure for Cloud-Scale Efficiency

Beyond Microsoft 365, Copilot's integration with Microsoft Azure further amplifies its capabilities, particularly for organizations with large-scale operations. Azure's cloud services allow Copilot to tap into powerful computing resources, enabling it to process vast amounts of data and run complex machine learning models.

For organizations dealing with large datasets or requiring high computational power, Azure provides the backend infrastructure that makes Copilot's insights even more powerful. This integration allows Copilot to offer more advanced AI capabilities, such as predictive analytics, natural language understanding, and real-time decision support, all powered by Azure's scalable infrastructure. Additionally, businesses can leverage Azure's security features, ensuring that sensitive information handled by Copilot is protected at all times.

Copilot's integration with Azure also enhances automation and artificial intelligence. For instance, it can monitor Azure services in real-time, suggesting improvements or notifying users of potential issues, all while helping businesses remain agile and responsive to changing conditions.

Leveraging AI Models and Insights from Microsoft Research

Microsoft's deep investment in AI research significantly enhances Copilot's capabilities. By integrating advanced models developed by Microsoft Research, Copilot is able to offer users access to cutting-edge AI technologies that are continuously improving. These models range from natural language processing to computer vision and predictive analytics, and they are used to enrich Copilot's functionality.

For example, Copilot's ability to understand and respond to complex queries in natural language is backed by Microsoft's advancements in natural language processing (NLP). These models are continuously trained on vast amounts of data, which helps them improve over time and handle a broader range of user requests. As new AI models are developed, Copilot will be able to integrate them seamlessly, ensuring that users always have access to the latest and most advanced features.

Future Outlook: Expanding the Ecosystem

As Microsoft continues to refine Copilot, its integration across the entire Microsoft ecosystem will likely deepen, further enhancing productivity. The vision for Copilot is to create a fully connected experience that allows users to switch between apps and platforms without friction, with each interaction tailored to their specific needs and workflow.

Looking forward, we can expect Copilot to integrate with more third-party tools, APIs, and services, creating a truly unified ecosystem that enhances productivity and collaboration. Microsoft's commitment to AI research and innovation ensures that Copilot will continue to evolve and expand, providing users with increasingly sophisticated capabilities that will redefine what it means to be productive in the modern workplace.

Chapter: Copilot in Data Analytics and Decision-Making

In the modern business environment, data is one of the most valuable assets an organization can possess. However, the ability to extract meaningful insights from vast amounts of data remains a complex and often time-consuming task. Microsoft Copilot is revolutionizing how businesses approach data analytics, enabling users to derive actionable insights from their data with minimal effort and expertise.

Intuitive Data Querying with Natural Language

One of the most compelling features of Copilot is its ability to process data using natural language queries. Instead of relying on traditional data science expertise to create complex queries, users can now simply ask questions in plain language, and Copilot will understand the context, retrieve the relevant data, and present it in a meaningful way. This drastically reduces the learning curve associated with data analytics, empowering non-technical users to harness the power of data.

For example, a sales manager might ask, "What were the top-performing products in the last quarter?" Copilot would immediately parse through the data, retrieve relevant figures, and present a clear, actionable report. This capability extends to more complex questions such as predictive analytics or time-series forecasting. With Copilot, users can request insights like, "What is the predicted sales growth for next quarter based on current trends?" and receive accurate predictions derived from historical data.

Advanced Visual Analytics and Reporting

Once Copilot has processed the data and generated insights, it can also assist with creating sophisticated visualizations. Using tools like Excel, Power BI, and even within PowerPoint for presentations, Copilot can create graphs, charts, and dashboards that allow users to better understand the data and communicate insights to others. Copilot's ability to generate these visualizations automatically based on user queries means that users no longer have to manually select chart types or struggle with the formatting of data visuals.

Whether creating an interactive dashboard in Power BI or generating a quick bar graph in Excel, Copilot ensures that the visuals are both accurate and aligned with the user's needs. By automating this process, Copilot significantly reduces the time spent on manual reporting and ensures that analytics can be easily interpreted by everyone, regardless of their data expertise.

Automated Insights for Business Decision-Making

Copilot's integration with advanced data analytics tools not only makes the data querying process more efficient but also introduces a layer of intelligent decision-making. With access to large datasets and advanced AI algorithms, Copilot can automatically generate insights, trends, and actionable recommendations. For example, in the context of business intelligence, Copilot might suggest potential business actions based on data patterns it detects, such as "You should consider expanding into the European market based on the current performance of your products in similar regions."

This ability to automate decision-making based on real-time data analysis is transforming the way businesses approach strategic planning. Copilot helps decision-makers at all levels—whether they are high-level executives or operational staff—make informed choices backed by data-driven insights.

Predictive and Prescriptive Analytics

In addition to descriptive analytics, which focuses on explaining past data, Copilot can also help organizations with predictive and prescriptive analytics. Predictive analytics allows businesses to forecast future outcomes based on historical data, while prescriptive analytics goes a step further by suggesting actions to optimize those outcomes.

Using Copilot, a retail manager might request, "What will be the expected demand for our products next holiday season?" Copilot can generate predictions based on seasonal trends, previous years' sales data, and current market conditions. Furthermore, it can recommend strategies such as adjusting inventory levels or launching targeted marketing campaigns based on predicted demand.

The power of predictive and prescriptive analytics is transforming industries, enabling businesses to proactively adjust strategies before problems arise or opportunities are missed.

Optimizing Operational Efficiency through Data Insights

Copilot's ability to process and analyze data doesn't stop at business intelligence. It extends to operational efficiency as well, particularly in industries such as manufacturing, supply chain, and logistics. By analyzing production data, supply chain metrics, and operational performance, Copilot can provide actionable recommendations to optimize processes, reduce waste, and enhance overall efficiency.

For example, in a manufacturing plant, Copilot can analyze machinery data to predict maintenance needs, allowing for predictive maintenance that reduces downtime. Similarly, in logistics, Copilot can analyze shipping patterns and make suggestions for route optimization or inventory management improvements.

In essence, Copilot's data-driven insights serve as a catalyst for smarter business decisions, driving efficiency, profitability, and competitive advantage across multiple industries.

Chapter: Enhancing Customer Support and Service Operations

Customer support and service operations are the front lines of any business, and ensuring that customers have positive experiences is crucial to long-term success. Microsoft Copilot is transforming customer service by integrating AI-powered capabilities that not only improve response times but also enhance the quality of support interactions.

AI-Driven Chatbots and Virtual Assistants

One of the most prominent applications of Copilot in customer support is the creation and management of AI-powered chatbots and virtual assistants. Traditionally, chatbots were rule-based systems that could only respond to a limited set of pre-programmed queries. However, with the advancement of natural language processing and machine learning, Copilot-powered chatbots can now engage in more fluid, natural conversations with customers, understanding context, and providing personalized assistance.

For instance, when a customer contacts support via chat, Copilot can automatically analyze the context of the inquiry, retrieve the most relevant information from databases or previous conversations, and suggest personalized solutions in real-time. Copilot is capable of handling a wide range of inquiries, from technical support to billing questions, without requiring human intervention. This reduces wait times and ensures that customers get the help they need quickly.

Moreover, these virtual assistants can continuously learn and adapt, improving over time as they engage with more customers and accumulate more data. This capability allows customer support systems to be constantly refined and enhanced, leading to better user experiences and higher customer satisfaction.

Omnichannel Support and Integration

As businesses increasingly offer customer support across multiple channels—email, chat, social media, voice calls, and more—copilot's ability to integrate these channels into a single, unified interface is crucial. Copilot enables agents to seamlessly switch between customer interactions on different platforms, ensuring that all customer data is synced and easily accessible. Whether a customer reaches out through email, social media, or chat, Copilot can provide agents with the context and history of the conversation, ensuring a seamless and personalized experience.

Additionally, Copilot can manage workflows across different communication channels. For example, if a customer initiates a query via chat and later follows up via email, Copilot ensures that the agent has access to the full context of the conversation, preventing customers from having to repeat themselves or wait for a response. This omnichannel support enhances customer satisfaction and streamlines customer service operations.

Smart Ticketing and Case Management

Copilot's capabilities extend to smart ticketing and case management. When a customer submits a support request, Copilot can automatically categorize the ticket, prioritize it based on urgency, and assign it to the most appropriate agent based on their expertise. This reduces the time spent on manual sorting and ensures that tickets are handled efficiently.

Furthermore, Copilot can monitor open cases, identify trends or recurring issues, and suggest improvements to customer support workflows. For example, if multiple customers report the same problem, Copilot can automatically flag this as a high-priority issue and escalate it to a human agent or team for resolution.

Enhancing Self-Service Options

Self-service is becoming an increasingly important aspect of customer support, as customers prefer to find answers to their questions without waiting for an agent. Copilot empowers organizations to develop more sophisticated self-service portals and knowledge bases. By using AI, Copilot can analyze customer queries and automatically update knowledge articles to ensure they remain relevant and accurate.

Copilot also assists in personalizing self-service options. For example, if a customer visits a knowledge base, Copilot can suggest articles or FAQs that are specifically relevant to their current issue, based on their browsing history or previous interactions. This proactive approach to self-service enhances the customer experience and reduces the need for live support.

Improving Agent Productivity

While Copilot excels at automating many aspects of customer support, it also works to enhance the productivity of human agents. By analyzing customer interactions and offering real-time suggestions, Copilot can help agents resolve issues faster and more effectively. For example, when an agent is engaged in a customer interaction, Copilot can provide contextual information, suggest responses, or offer relevant solutions that the agent may not have considered.

Additionally, Copilot can handle repetitive administrative tasks such as updating customer records, logging interactions, and processing tickets, freeing agents to focus on more complex issues that require human intervention. This leads to faster resolution times and greater job satisfaction for support teams, as they are relieved from monotonous tasks.

Chapter: Copilot and AI Ethics in Business Operations

As artificial intelligence becomes increasingly integrated into business operations, ethical considerations become an essential aspect of its deployment. Microsoft Copilot, like other AI systems, raises important questions about transparency, fairness, privacy, and accountability. Understanding how to use Copilot responsibly is crucial to ensuring that AI is leveraged in ways that benefit both organizations and their stakeholders.

Transparency and Explainability

One of the primary ethical concerns surrounding AI is the need for transparency and explainability. With complex AI models, such as those driving Copilot, it can be difficult for users to understand how decisions are made or why certain suggestions are offered. This is especially important in areas like hiring, lending, and healthcare, where AI-driven decisions can have significant consequences on individuals' lives.

Microsoft is committed to making its AI systems, including Copilot, more transparent. This includes providing clear information about how the AI works, how it was trained, and what data it uses to make decisions. Ensuring that AI systems are explainable not only helps users trust the technology but also ensures that businesses can justify AI-driven decisions when required.

Addressing Bias and Fairness

AI systems, including Copilot, are only as unbiased as the data they are trained on. If AI models are trained on biased data, they may unintentionally perpetuate inequalities. For instance, in the context of hiring, if Copilot is trained on historical hiring data that reflects biases against certain groups, the system may unintentionally discriminate against these groups.

Microsoft is actively working to mitigate bias in its AI systems, including Copilot. This includes using diverse datasets, implementing bias-detection tools, and continuously evaluating the system's outputs to ensure fairness. Copilot's ability to flag biased patterns or offer suggestions for bias mitigation is an essential aspect of ensuring that AI technology is used in ways that are fair and equitable.

Ensuring Privacy and Data Security

The ethical use of AI also involves protecting individuals' privacy and ensuring that data is used responsibly. Copilot's integration with tools like Microsoft Azure means that businesses must be mindful of how customer data is handled, stored, and shared. Copilot helps businesses comply with data protection regulations such as GDPR by offering features like data anonymization and encryption.

By prioritizing privacy and security, Microsoft ensures that Copilot can be used responsibly without compromising the sensitive information of customers, employees, or other stakeholders. Additionally, users can configure Copilot's privacy settings to align with their organization's specific data security requirements.

Chapter: The Future of Copilot and AI-Driven Business Transformation

The capabilities of Microsoft Copilot represent just the beginning of what is possible when AI and business operations intersect. As AI technology continues to evolve, so too will the scope and potential applications of Copilot.

Expanding Copilot's Capabilities

Microsoft is continually improving Copilot's capabilities, with advancements in natural language processing, machine learning, and data analytics. The future of Copilot will see even deeper integrations with enterprise systems, more sophisticated decision-

making algorithms, and greater personalization.

For example, future versions of Copilot could offer

even more proactive recommendations based on data

analysis, helping businesses anticipate challenges and

seize opportunities before they arise. Furthermore,

Copilot's ability to learn from individual user

preferences will allow it to offer more tailored

experiences, further enhancing productivity and user

satisfaction.

Integrating with Emerging Technologies

Looking ahead, Copilot will likely integrate with

emerging technologies such as quantum computing,

5G, and the Internet of Things (IoT). These

advancements will allow Copilot to process larger datasets, generate more accurate predictions, and deliver more powerful insights in real-time.

For instance, Copilot could leverage quantum computing to solve complex optimization problems that are currently beyond the reach of traditional computing, providing businesses with unprecedented analytical capabilities.

AI for Social Good

As businesses adopt AI-powered tools like Copilot, they will also have the opportunity to contribute to social good. Copilot's capabilities can be harnessed to address societal challenges, such as climate change, poverty, and healthcare access. By analyzing vast amounts of data, Copilot can help organizations identify opportunities for social impact, streamline operations, and make more informed decisions that benefit both their bottom line and society.

As the use of AI continues to grow, Microsoft Copilot will play a critical role in transforming how businesses operate, engage with customers, and leverage technology to drive both innovation and positive change.

Chapter: Copilot in Product Development and Innovation

In today's rapidly evolving marketplace, innovation is crucial to maintaining a competitive edge. Microsoft Copilot is enabling businesses to enhance their product development processes by integrating AI into every phase of the product lifecycle. From ideation to prototyping to market launch, Copilot provides tools that streamline and accelerate innovation.

Accelerating Ideation and Conceptualization

The first stage of product development involves brainstorming and generating ideas that meet market needs. Copilot can assist teams in this phase by analyzing market trends, consumer feedback, and competitor products to identify gaps in the market. Copilot can suggest new product ideas or features based on real-time data and previous successful innovations, helping businesses stay ahead of trends and customer demands.

For example, in a consumer electronics company, Copilot might analyze data from social media, online reviews, and product usage to suggest features that users are asking for but are currently missing from the product offerings. It could also generate potential product names or slogans based on keyword trends, optimizing the chances of success in the market.

Streamlining Prototyping and Testing

Once the idea phase is complete, the next step in product development is creating prototypes and testing them for functionality and market viability. Copilot can help streamline this phase by aiding in the design and testing processes. By leveraging machine learning and AI-driven simulations, Copilot can automatically generate design prototypes, predict potential failures, and suggest improvements before the physical prototype is even created.

Additionally, Copilot can assist with user testing by analyzing feedback from focus groups or early testers. By processing qualitative and quantitative feedback, Copilot can identify patterns in user experiences and recommend adjustments to product features or user interfaces. This process reduces the need for multiple rounds of physical testing, saving both time and resources.

Optimizing Product Launch and Market Fit

When it's time to launch a new product, Copilot provides businesses with tools to ensure market fit and maximize the success of the launch. It can analyze customer sentiment from various data sources like reviews, surveys, and social media to gauge how well the product is being received and whether adjustments are necessary.

Moreover, Copilot can assist in demand forecasting by leveraging historical data and trends to predict the level of interest in the product and recommend inventory levels, marketing strategies, and sales tactics. This enables businesses to scale production and marketing efforts in line with expected demand, optimizing the product's introduction to the market.

AI-Driven Continuous Improvement

Even after a product has launched, Copilot's capabilities continue to add value. Using feedback loops from customers and internal systems, Copilot can provide recommendations for iterative improvements to the product. This could involve suggesting software updates, proposing new features based on user requests, or highlighting areas where customer satisfaction is lacking.

By continuously analyzing product performance and customer feedback, Copilot helps businesses stay agile, ensuring that their products evolve in line with changing customer needs and market conditions.

Chapter: Copilot in Human Resources and Talent Management

Human resources (HR) is another area that is benefiting greatly from the integration of AI technologies like Microsoft Copilot. By automating administrative tasks and providing data-driven insights, Copilot enables HR teams to focus more on strategic initiatives such as talent development, retention, and organizational growth.

AI-Powered Recruitment and Talent Sourcing

Copilot can assist with the recruitment process by analyzing resumes and applications to identify the best candidates for open positions. Using natural language processing (NLP), Copilot can scan resumes, cover letters, and LinkedIn profiles to detect key qualifications, experiences, and skills that match the job description.

Beyond simply filtering applications, Copilot can also assess the fit of candidates based on company culture and diversity goals. It can help reduce bias in the recruitment process by ensuring that candidates are selected based on objective criteria rather than subjective judgments. For instance, Copilot can suggest candidates who might have been overlooked by traditional hiring managers, ensuring a more diverse and inclusive hiring process.

Enhancing Employee Onboarding

Once candidates are hired, Copilot can streamline the onboarding process by providing personalized training materials, company policies, and process guides. Using machine learning algorithms, Copilot can tailor onboarding content to each employee's role and learning style, ensuring that the process is engaging and effective.

Furthermore, Copilot can automate the completion of routine paperwork, compliance training, and policy acknowledgment, allowing HR professionals to focus on higher-value tasks. By simplifying and personalizing the onboarding process, Copilot ensures new hires are better prepared and more likely to succeed in their roles.

Employee Engagement and Performance Management

Keeping employees engaged and motivated is essential for organizational success. Copilot helps HR departments track and assess employee performance through continuous monitoring of work outputs, feedback, and peer reviews. Using sentiment analysis,

Copilot can detect shifts in employee morale and engagement, identifying potential areas of concern before they escalate.

Additionally, Copilot assists in performance management by providing managers with data-driven insights on employee productivity, skill development, and career progression. It can recommend personalized learning and development programs to help employees improve and grow within the company, ensuring long-term retention.

Retention Strategies and Predictive Analytics

Employee turnover is one of the most significant costs for any organization. Copilot leverages predictive analytics to help HR professionals anticipate which employees might be at risk of leaving the company. By analyzing factors such as job satisfaction, compensation, tenure, and career progression, Copilot can identify employees who may be likely to leave and recommend retention strategies.

These strategies could include targeted interventions such as career coaching, skill development opportunities, or even adjustments to compensation packages. By proactively addressing employee concerns, Copilot helps businesses reduce turnover and retain top talent.

Chapter: Copilot in Marketing and Customer Relationship Management

Microsoft Copilot is transforming marketing strategies by providing AI-driven tools to create more personalized, effective campaigns that engage customers across multiple touchpoints. From customer segmentation to content creation, Copilot enables marketers to optimize their efforts and deliver better results.

Customer Segmentation and Targeting

One of the key aspects of any marketing strategy is identifying the right target audience. Copilot uses machine learning algorithms to analyze customer data and segment audiences based on demographic information, behaviors, and purchasing patterns. By understanding customer preferences, Copilot can create more accurate customer profiles and recommend tailored marketing strategies for each segment.

For example, Copilot might suggest creating a targeted email campaign for a segment of customers who have previously purchased high-end electronics but have not made a purchase in the last six months. This type of segmentation allows marketers to send more relevant and personalized messages, increasing the likelihood of conversion.

Content Creation and Personalization

Copilot can also assist in content creation by generating tailored marketing materials, including social media posts, email newsletters, and even ad copy. By analyzing historical performance data, Copilot learns which types of content resonate most with specific customer segments and uses that data to create content that is more likely to drive engagement.

In addition to generating content, Copilot personalizes marketing messages based on customer preferences, behavior, and past interactions. For example, it might suggest sending an exclusive discount to customers who have shown interest in a particular product category but haven't yet made a purchase. This

personalized approach enhances the customer
experience and boosts conversion rates.

Campaign Management and Optimization

Copilot's capabilities extend to campaign
management, where it can track the performance of
marketing efforts in real time. By continuously
analyzing data from various marketing channels—such
as email, social media, and paid ads—Copilot can
provide actionable insights to optimize campaigns.
This includes adjusting ad spend, tweaking messaging,
or changing targeting strategies based on
performance metrics.

For instance, if a social media ad campaign is
underperforming, Copilot might recommend adjusting

the target audience or revising the messaging to better align with customer interests. These real-time optimizations ensure that marketing budgets are spent effectively, maximizing return on investment (ROI).

Customer Relationship Management (CRM)

Customer relationship management is another area where Copilot shines. By integrating with CRM platforms such as Dynamics 365, Copilot provides sales and marketing teams with a unified view of customer interactions and preferences. Copilot's AI-powered insights help identify potential leads, upsell opportunities, and retention strategies.

Copilot can also assist in automating routine CRM tasks, such as sending follow-up emails, scheduling meetings, or tracking customer inquiries. By automating these tasks, sales and marketing teams can focus on building stronger, more personalized relationships with their customers, ultimately improving customer loyalty and lifetime value.

Chapter: Copilot for Financial Analysis and Management

Finance is one of the most data-intensive areas of any business, and Microsoft Copilot is helping finance teams work more efficiently by automating routine

tasks, providing real-time analytics, and generating
financial forecasts and insights.

Automated Financial Reporting and Analysis

Financial reporting is a critical function in any
organization, but it often involves repetitive tasks
such as data entry, reconciliation, and report
generation. Copilot automates these tasks by pulling
data from various sources, performing calculations,
and generating financial reports that are accurate and
up-to-date. This saves finance professionals significant
time and ensures that reports are always aligned with
the latest data.

For example, Copilot can automatically generate
income statements, balance sheets, and cash flow

reports based on real-time data from accounting software, eliminating the need for manual data entry. It can also provide variance analysis, highlighting discrepancies between actual and budgeted financials, helping finance teams quickly identify areas that need attention.

Financial Forecasting and Predictive Analytics

Forecasting is an essential part of financial management, and Copilot helps improve the accuracy of financial forecasts by analyzing historical data, market trends, and external economic factors. Copilot's AI algorithms predict future revenue, expenses, cash flow, and other financial metrics, allowing businesses to make more informed decisions.

For example, Copilot can predict cash flow shortages based on trends and recommend adjustments such as delaying capital expenditures or tightening credit terms to avoid potential liquidity issues. This proactive approach to financial management ensures that businesses are better prepared for future financial challenges.

Risk Management and Compliance

Copilot assists finance teams in managing risk by analyzing financial data for potential threats, such as fraud, misreporting, or market volatility. It can flag unusual transactions or deviations from established financial norms, providing an early warning system for potential risks.

Additionally, Copilot ensures that financial activities comply with regulatory requirements by keeping track of changing regulations and automatically adjusting reports to meet the latest standards. For instance, it can help businesses ensure compliance with tax laws, accounting standards, or financial disclosures, reducing the risk of costly fines or penalties.

Budgeting and Cost Optimization

Managing budgets and controlling costs are ongoing challenges for finance teams. Copilot assists by providing detailed analysis of spending patterns, suggesting cost-saving measures, and tracking budget performance in real time. By analyzing data from across the organization, Copilot identifies inefficiencies and suggests areas where spending can be reduced without sacrificing operational effectiveness.

For example, Copilot might identify an underutilized software subscription or highlight opportunities to negotiate better pricing with vendors. By optimizing costs, businesses can improve profitability and reinvest savings into growth initiatives.

Chapter: Copilot for Supply Chain Optimization

Supply chains are the backbone of most businesses, and optimizing them is essential for ensuring efficiency, cost-effectiveness, and customer satisfaction. Microsoft Copilot is transforming supply chain management by providing real-time insights, predictive analytics, and automation to streamline operations.

Supply Chain Visibility and Real-Time Analytics

Copilot helps businesses gain end-to-end visibility into their supply chain by integrating with various data sources, including inventory management systems, shipping providers, and supplier databases. By processing this data in real time, Copilot provides managers with a comprehensive view of the entire supply chain, helping them identify bottlenecks, delays, and inefficiencies.

For example, Copilot can detect a delay in raw materials delivery and suggest alternative suppliers to minimize production disruptions. It can also track inventory levels in real time, alerting supply chain managers when stock is running low or when excess inventory needs to be reduced.

Demand Forecasting and Inventory Management

Accurate demand forecasting is a key component of supply chain optimization. Copilot leverages historical sales data, market trends, and external factors such as seasonality and economic conditions to predict future demand for products. By providing more accurate forecasts, Copilot helps businesses reduce the risk of overstocking or stockouts.

For instance, Copilot can recommend optimal inventory levels for each product based on forecasted demand, ensuring that businesses have enough stock to meet customer needs without overinvesting in inventory. This helps reduce storage costs and improve cash flow.

Supplier Relationship Management

Managing supplier relationships is another critical aspect of supply chain management. Copilot can analyze supplier performance data, track delivery timelines, and assess the quality of goods or services provided. Using this data, Copilot can suggest ways to improve relationships with suppliers, such as negotiating better terms or finding new suppliers who offer better pricing or reliability.

In case of disruptions, Copilot can suggest alternate suppliers and help maintain continuity of supply, ensuring that businesses are less vulnerable to external shocks.

Logistics Optimization and Cost Reduction

Optimizing logistics is essential for reducing supply chain costs and improving delivery times. Copilot can analyze data from transportation systems to identify inefficiencies and suggest ways to optimize routes, reduce shipping costs, or improve delivery schedules. By analyzing real-time data on weather, traffic, and logistics costs, Copilot helps companies make smarter decisions about how to move goods and services.

By leveraging AI to optimize supply chain processes, Copilot helps businesses reduce costs, increase efficiency, and ultimately improve customer

satisfaction through faster and more reliable
deliveries.

Chapter 6: Copilot in Outlook: Effective Communication

Drowning in emails? Copilot in Outlook can be your
lifeline. This chapter explores how Copilot streamlines
communication and information overload:

- **6.1 Summarizing Emails and Managing Inbox:**
  Get a handle on your inbox with ease:

- Automatically summarize lengthy emails and identify key points.
- Utilize Copilot's suggestions for prioritizing emails and organizing your inbox efficiently.
- Leverage automated filtering and labeling to manage email flow.

- **6.2 Composing Drafts with Suggested Tone and Length:** Craft professional and impactful emails:
  - Receive suggestions on tone and style to ensure appropriate communication in your emails.
  - Maintain a concise and focused writing style with Copilot's length recommendations.

- Utilize pre-built templates and greetings tailored to different email scenarios.

- **6.3 Scheduling and Meeting Management Support:** Effortlessly manage your schedule and meetings:

  - Schedule meetings with suggested times based on attendee availability.

  - Generate automated meeting agendas and summaries with Copilot's assistance.

  - Utilize Copilot to follow up on action items and tasks after meetings.

Chapter 7: Copilot in Teams: Improved Collaboration

Boost teamwork and project management with Copilot's collaborative features within Microsoft Teams:

- **7.1 Real-Time Meeting Transcripts and Summaries:** Ensure everyone stays on the same page:
  - Generate real-time transcripts of meetings within Teams for easy reference.

- Utilize Copilot to automatically create summaries of key decisions and action items.

- Improve accessibility for participants who might miss parts of the meeting.

- **7.2 Action Item Management and Task Delegation:** Maintain project structure and accountability:

  - Assign tasks and action items directly within Teams conversations with Copilot's guidance.

  - Track progress on tasks and deadlines with automated reminders and notifications.

- Delegate tasks efficiently and ensure clear ownership within your team.

- **7.3 Brainstorming and Creative Collaboration Tools:** Spark innovation and generate ideas together:

  - Utilize Copilot's suggestion features for brainstorming activities and mind maps.

  - Facilitate collaborative content creation within Teams documents with real-time co-editing.

  - Encourage creative thinking and problem-solving within your team.

Case Study 1: Copilot for Financial Forecasting in a Global Corporation

Background:

XYZ Corporation is a multinational company operating in the manufacturing sector, with production facilities across the globe. The company's financial forecasting process was largely manual, relying on Excel spreadsheets and static historical data. This led to delays, inaccuracies, and inefficiencies, making it difficult to respond swiftly to market changes.

Challenge:

The company needed a more accurate and responsive method for forecasting its financials, particularly in terms of revenue and expenditure across different markets. With fluctuating demand, exchange rates, and geopolitical risks, the company struggled to predict financial outcomes effectively, which impacted its ability to make strategic decisions.

Solution:

XYZ Corporation integrated Microsoft Copilot into its financial forecasting process, using its AI-powered capabilities to automate data collection and analysis. Copilot integrated data from internal systems such as sales, operations, and HR, along with external data sources, including economic indicators and industry trends. By using machine learning, Copilot was able to predict revenue, costs, and profitability with a higher degree of accuracy.

For example, Copilot analyzed historical data on raw material costs and global trade trends, identifying patterns that had previously gone unnoticed. This enabled the company to predict price changes in raw materials and adjust forecasts for production costs, providing a more dynamic financial outlook.

Results:

After implementing Copilot, XYZ Corporation saw a significant reduction in the time required for financial forecasting. The process, which previously took weeks, was now completed in days. Forecast accuracy improved by 20%, allowing the finance team to proactively address potential issues such as cash flow shortages and budget overruns. Copilot also provided real-time scenario analysis, enabling leadership to explore various "what-if" scenarios, such as changes in demand, exchange rates, or raw material prices, and assess their potential impact on profitability.

Additionally, Copilot helped the company identify inefficiencies in its cost structure, resulting in an overall 15% reduction in operating expenses. The automation of financial processes allowed the finance team to focus on more strategic tasks, such as long-term planning and investment analysis.

Conclusion:

Microsoft Copilot significantly enhanced XYZ Corporation's financial forecasting capabilities. By automating data integration and leveraging predictive analytics, the company was able to make more

informed, data-driven decisions, improving its

financial agility and competitiveness.

Case Study 2: Copilot for Risk Management in Banking

Background:

ABC Bank is a large financial institution that serves millions of customers globally. As a critical part of its operations, the bank must continually monitor and manage risks such as fraud, regulatory non-compliance, and market volatility. Traditionally, the risk management process was siloed, with teams manually analyzing data from various sources, which was time-consuming and prone to human error.

Challenge:

ABC Bank needed to enhance its risk management practices, particularly in fraud detection and regulatory compliance. The bank faced growing challenges in identifying fraudulent transactions in real-time and ensuring compliance with evolving global regulations.

Solution:

ABC Bank deployed Microsoft Copilot to streamline its risk management processes. Copilot integrated with the bank's core systems and external data feeds to continuously monitor transactions and flag suspicious activity. Using AI, Copilot analyzed patterns in transaction history to identify anomalies that could indicate fraud, such as unusual spending behavior or mismatched transaction data.

For regulatory compliance, Copilot was used to automatically generate reports aligned with international regulations, such as the EU's GDPR and the US's Dodd-Frank Act. By keeping track of changing laws and regulations, Copilot ensured the bank's operations remained compliant without requiring manual intervention.

Results:

The implementation of Copilot led to a dramatic reduction in fraudulent activities, with the system identifying and flagging suspicious transactions 30% faster than the previous manual process. The AI-driven alerts allowed risk managers to investigate and address issues before they became serious problems. Copilot's ability to spot emerging fraud patterns in real-time helped the bank reduce fraud losses by 18%.

Furthermore, Copilot's automated compliance reporting saved the bank countless hours each month, reducing the manual effort involved in creating compliance documents by 40%. The bank's legal and compliance teams were able to focus on higher-level tasks, such as strategy development, rather than routine reporting.

Conclusion:

With Microsoft Copilot, ABC Bank successfully transformed its risk management practices. The AI-powered system improved fraud detection,

streamlined regulatory compliance, and provided a

more efficient way to manage risks, helping the bank

reduce operational losses and enhance its reputation.

Case Study 3: Copilot for Customer Support Automation in Retail

Background:

DEF Retail is a global retailer that operates both online and in physical stores. As its customer base grew, the company faced an increasing volume of customer service inquiries, which were handled by a large team of support agents. Despite their efforts, response times were slow, and customer satisfaction began to decline.

Challenge:

DEF Retail needed a solution to improve its customer support efficiency while maintaining a high level of service. The company sought to automate routine customer inquiries and provide faster, more personalized responses to complex issues.

Solution:

DEF Retail integrated Microsoft Copilot into its customer support platform. Copilot's natural language processing (NLP) capabilities allowed it to analyze customer inquiries and provide automated, intelligent responses. The system was trained to recognize common issues such as order status requests, product availability, and return policies, which it could handle autonomously.

For more complex queries, Copilot assisted support agents by providing real-time suggestions based on the customer's history and context, allowing agents to respond more quickly and accurately.

Results:

After deploying Copilot, DEF Retail saw a 40% reduction in the average response time for customer inquiries. Routine queries were resolved by Copilot without needing human intervention, allowing support agents to focus on more complex issues. Customer satisfaction improved by 25%, as customers were able to receive quick answers to common questions and more personalized responses to unique issues.

Additionally, Copilot's data-driven insights enabled the company to identify recurring customer pain points, leading to improvements in product offerings and service policies. This proactive approach enhanced both customer loyalty and operational efficiency.

Conclusion:

Microsoft Copilot transformed DEF Retail's customer support operations, enabling faster, more efficient service while freeing up human agents to handle more complex issues. By leveraging AI-powered automation, the company was able to improve customer satisfaction and streamline its support workflows.

Case Study 4: Copilot for Supply Chain Optimization in Manufacturing

Background:

GHI Manufacturing is a leading producer of consumer electronics with a global supply chain. The company faced challenges with supply chain inefficiencies, including delays in sourcing raw materials, fluctuating inventory levels, and increased logistics costs.

Challenge:

GHI Manufacturing needed a solution to optimize its supply chain operations, ensuring timely production and minimizing costs. The company required better visibility into its supply chain to proactively address issues and reduce operational bottlenecks.

Solution:

GHI Manufacturing implemented Microsoft Copilot to gain real-time insights into its supply chain. Copilot integrated data from suppliers, inventory systems, and logistics providers to provide a comprehensive view of the entire supply chain. It identified delays in raw material deliveries and suggested alternative suppliers to ensure continuity of production.

Copilot also used historical sales data and market trends to predict demand more accurately, allowing GHI Manufacturing to optimize inventory levels and reduce excess stock.

Results:

Copilot helped GHI Manufacturing reduce lead times by 15%, ensuring that production schedules were met more consistently. By optimizing inventory management, the company was able to reduce stockouts by 20%, improving product availability for customers.

In logistics, Copilot identified inefficiencies in shipping routes, leading to a 10% reduction in transportation costs. The predictive capabilities of Copilot also helped the company prepare for fluctuations in demand, minimizing the risk of overstocking and reducing storage costs.

Conclusion:

Microsoft Copilot played a pivotal role in optimizing GHI Manufacturing's supply chain. By providing real-time visibility, improving demand forecasting, and optimizing logistics, the company achieved cost savings, improved operational efficiency, and better customer satisfaction.

Case Study 5: Copilot for Marketing Campaign Optimization

Background:

JKL Media is a global advertising agency specializing in digital marketing. The company managed multiple client campaigns, often running into challenges with tracking performance across channels, optimizing spend, and measuring ROI in real time.

Challenge:

JKL Media needed a tool to streamline campaign management, allowing them to optimize ad spend and measure the effectiveness of campaigns more accurately. The company wanted to ensure that clients were getting the best return on investment (ROI) for their advertising dollars.

Solution:

JKL Media integrated Microsoft Copilot into their marketing analytics tools. Copilot's ability to aggregate data from various advertising platforms such as Google Ads, Facebook, and Twitter allowed the agency to track campaign performance in real time. Copilot used machine learning to identify patterns and suggest optimizations, such as reallocating ad budgets to the best-performing channels or adjusting ad creatives for better engagement.

Copilot also provided detailed reports on campaign performance, highlighting key metrics like customer acquisition cost (CAC), lifetime value (LTV), and conversion rates.

Results:

With Copilot's AI-powered recommendations, JKL Media was able to optimize ad spend, increasing ROI by 25%. The ability to track and adjust campaigns in real time led to better targeting and improved performance across all channels. Clients were more satisfied with the results, and the agency gained a reputation for delivering high-impact, data-driven campaigns.

Conclusion:

Microsoft Copilot enabled JKL Media to enhance the efficiency and effectiveness of its marketing campaigns. By providing real-time insights and intelligent recommendations, Copilot helped the agency deliver superior results to its clients, increasing

both satisfaction and profitability.

Part 3: Advanced Features and Customization

This section dives into the world of fine-tuning Copilot

for your specific needs and exploring its potential for

developers.

Chapter 8: Customizing Copilot Settings for Optimal Use

Unlock Copilot's full potential by tailoring it to your work style and preferences. This chapter explores:

- **8.1 Tailoring Suggestions to Your Workflow:**

  Make Copilot work for you:

  - Adjust the level of detail and complexity in Copilot's suggestions.

  - Train Copilot on your writing style and frequently used phrases for personalized recommendations.

- Set specific preferences for grammar, tone, and formatting to ensure Copilot aligns with your needs.

- **8.2 Integrating Third-Party Applications:**

Expand Copilot's capabilities:

- Connect Copilot with other productivity tools and services you use.

- Streamline workflows by allowing Copilot to access data and information from external applications.

- Explore a growing ecosystem of integrations to further enhance your productivity.

- **8.3 Providing Feedback and Improving Copilot:**

Be part of the evolution:

- Provide feedback on Copilot's suggestions to improve its accuracy and relevance.

- Report bugs or unexpected behavior to contribute to the ongoing development of Copilot.

- Help shape the future of AI-powered assistance by actively participating in user feedback mechanisms.

Chapter 9: Exploring the Potential of Copilot for Developers

For developers, Copilot offers a powerful new paradigm for coding. This chapter delves into:

- **9.1 Code Completion and Suggestion Features:** Write code faster and more efficiently:
  - Leverage Copilot's ability to suggest entire lines of code, functions, and class definitions.
  - Utilize context-aware suggestions that adapt to your existing code structure.
  - Reduce boilerplate code and repetitive tasks with Copilot's automation.
- **9.2 Integration with Development Tools and IDEs:** Seamless workflow within your coding environment:

- Explore how Copilot integrates with popular IDEs (Integrated Development Environments) like Visual Studio Code.

- Utilize Copilot's features directly within your coding interface for a smooth workflow.

- Discover plugins and extensions that enhance Copilot's functionality within your preferred IDE.

- **9.3 Ethical Considerations and Responsible AI Practices:** Harness the power of AI responsibly:

  - Understand potential biases present in AI models and how they might influence Copilot's suggestions.

- Employ best practices for code security and maintain control over the code Copilot generates.
- Foster an environment of responsible AI development within your coding practices.

By mastering these advanced features, you can transform Copilot into an indispensable tool that streamlines your workflow and unlocks new levels of productivity in various aspects of your work.

Part 4: The Future of Copilot

This section explores the exciting possibilities on the horizon for Copilot and its potential impact on the way we work.

Chapter 10: Emerging Capabilities and Upcoming Developments

Get a glimpse into the future with this chapter on Copilot's ongoing evolution. We'll explore:

- **Advanced Personalization:** Expect Copilot to become even more attuned to your individual needs:

    - Context-aware understanding of your work goals and project requirements.

- The ability to learn from your past interactions and preferences for even more personalized suggestions.

- Integration with personal calendars and task management systems for seamless workflow management.

- **Enhanced Multi-Lingual Support:** Break down language barriers and expand collaboration possibilities:

  - Real-time translation capabilities within Copilot, allowing seamless communication and content creation across languages.

  - Multilingual content suggestions and research assistance, fostering global collaboration.

- The ability to translate entire documents and presentations while maintaining formatting and style.

- **Integration with Advanced AI Tools:** Unlock new levels of automation and intelligence:

  - Copilot's potential connection with AI-powered research tools for in-depth analysis and data exploration.

  - Integration with creative AI models for generating unique design concepts and marketing materials.

  - The ability to leverage AI for automated project management and resource allocation based on real-time data.

Chapter 11: The Impact of Copilot on Workstyles and Industries

This chapter explores the transformative potential of Copilot across various industries and professions. We'll discuss:

- **Shifting Workstyles:** How Copilot might change the way we work:

- A potential increase in knowledge worker productivity, allowAing for a focus on higher-level tasks.

- The emergence of new job roles focused on managing and optimizing AI-powered workflows.

- A potential shift towards collaboration over individual work as communication and information sharing become more streamlined.

- **Industry-Specific Applications:** The tailored impact of Copilot on different sectors:

  - Revolutionizing content creation and marketing with automated ad copy

generation and data-driven content
strategies.

- o Transforming research and development
  through AI-powered data analysis and
  scientific paper generation.

- o Enhancing customer service experiences
  with Copilot-powered chatbots and
  personalized communication tools.

By understanding the future trajectory of Copilot, you
can prepare yourself and your organization to
leverage its capabilities for continued success in the
ever-evolving work landscape.

www.ingramcontent.com/pod-product-compliance
Lightning Source LLC
LaVergne TN
LVHW051653050326
832903LV00032B/3793